LONDON IN THE THIRTIES

ALICE PROCHASKA

LONDON MUSEUM

London   Her Majesty's Stationery Office   1973

SBN 11 290170 0

PREFACE

London at the beginning of the thirties was the sprawling but powerful focal point of a Commonwealth of Nations whose relations, codified in the Statute of Westminster 1931, seemed to promise the most sophisticated form of internationalism devised by modern man. At the end of the decade it faced possible enemy occupation, probable destruction, and well-nigh certain exhaustion. The age was one of high hopes and social progress on the one hand, and of bitter poverty, nightmarish fears and deliberate self-deception on the other. These polarities are reflected in the present exhibition, which attempts to reconstitute not only the physical appearance of London in the thirties, but the complex aspirations and attitudes of mind of Londoners of all classes and from all walks of life. It is notoriously difficult to write (or display) recent history – for one thing events are difficult to keep in focus, for another the material to digest is so multifarious – but it is imperative for a historical museum to assess, collect and preserve contemporary material while it still can, and we hope that the exhibition will not only present a valid point of view but make as serious and permanent a contribution to our knowledge of London history as last summer's exhibition in the Museum, *Chaucer's London*.

The exhibition is the third in the current series devoted to life in London at different periods of its history, and has been the joint work of Alice Prochaska and Christopher Firmstone, whose lively collaboration has been a model of what the relationship between a curator and a designer ought to be. Alice Prochaska, who has worked with tireless enthusiasm, has been responsible for the administration as well as the historical research, scenario and labelling; Christopher Firmstone has brought the period vividly alive with his highly imaginative design and disposition of the material. I am grateful to them both for their achievement.

Once again we are deeply indebted to those many colleagues and private individuals who have so readily assisted us with loans and information; full acknowledgements will be found in the handlist accompanying this booklet, but I should like to place on record here my own appreciation of the kindness of these generous friends of the Museum. Without their help the enterprise could never have developed in the exciting way it did.

JOHN HAYES
Director

Kensington Palace, February 1973

1 Traffic near the Bank of England

2 The Jarrow marchers arriving in London on 31 October 1936

The thirties: a bleak decade in the recollection of many people, or for others a time when widening horizons and new material comforts made the Depression and threats of war seem unreal. The shade of the Second World War falls between us and our notion of the thirties, whether we lived through them or know them at second hand. Only with difficulty can we stand back from a decade that lies in a no-man's land between past and present, a piece of history where memory intrudes.

London in the thirties presents its full share of problems to the retrospective view. Confident and expanding, its wealth and size dominated Great Britain more than at any other time in the twentieth century. No other city could boast a greater range of occupations and interests amongst its inhabitants, nor offer them a wider or more dazzling choice of entertainment for their leisure; and yet it faced acute difficulties. From the 'distressed areas' hunger marchers converged on the capital to bring home their miserable plight to the country's most affluent community; but London itself contained areas of hopeless poverty. From abroad came news of disturbing political struggles which most Englishmen thought remote from their own experience; but too often Londoners saw them echoed in the streets and meeting-places of their own city. For the Londoner sitting at home in the evening with his newspaper or his wireless, it was not an easy state of affairs to understand.

3 *Children playing cricket in Alpha Road, Millwall*

4 Bedroom of a house in Church Street Chelsea, designed by Walter
Gropius and Maxwell Fry in 1934

HOME

A Londoner's home might be anything from one room in an insanitary slum house to a mansion in Mayfair or Belgravia, and in between the two extremes there existed huge variations. Many of the nineteenth-century terrace houses in Kensington, Chelsea or Bloomsbury for example, still housed single families with servants as they had been designed to do. The number of people entering domestic service in Britain as a whole had dropped dramatically to only five per cent of the population, but as the advertisement columns of *The Times* showed, there was still a demand for cooks, maids and nannies that reached far beyond the confines of the wealthy.

The typical town house belonging to a well-to-do family was arranged with kitchen, scullery and perhaps a maid's sitting room in the basement; and most probably a creaking dumb waiter of some antiquity would convey the food from kitchen to ground floor dining room. The kitchen itself might boast a rug and an armchair for the maid if she had no sitting-room, but otherwise it was cheerless. Electric washing machines were to be found in many middle-class London homes by this time, and so were refrigerators, giving rise to a new vogue for iced puddings. But sinks were still low enough to induce maximum backache in the washer-up, and lighting was poor. As for the rest of the house, the possibilities were legion. Continental and American visitors might be startled by the absence of central heating and the dearth of lampshades to mitigate the glare and novelty of electric lights; but standards of comfort had risen appreciably in London homes since 1918. Electric fires, lighting and cleaning equipment were catching on wherever family finances could stand the high price of electricity. After 1936, television was another luxury available to Londoners. And in many houses the influence of *avant-garde* design made inroads on the cluttered darkness of Edwardian taste.

The truly modern Londoner of means bought much of his furniture from Heal's; or else he ventured into the showrooms of one of the several excellent firms that produced functional,

5 *Gilded table lamp with frosted glass flower and marble base*

clean-lined furniture by designers like Marcel Breuer or Serge Chermayeff, to name two of many. He might be tempted to employ an interior decorator: if not one of the leading pioneers such as Curtis Moffatt, Syrie Maugham (wife of the novelist) or Sybil Colefax, then one of their numerous acolytes. Interior design at its best during the thirties was exciting and self-consciously modern. The influences of the Bauhaus from Germany and of art deco from France were both important in London; and other fashions from the continent included the Dutch 'de Stijl' and the Finnish furniture of Alvar Aalto. There were many British designers of note and originality, but their admirers formed a small group. When the Royal Academy broke with tradition and held a winter exhibition of 'Art in Industry' in 1935, the great majority of unfavourable reactions in the press reflected a prevailing conservatism. Even the taste for Victorian furnishings that the Sitwells had championed since the twenties was only just catching on.

The average Londoner setting up house during the thirties was unlikely to live in Kensington, Chelsea or Bloomsbury. His cook was his wife, his house one of the new ones going up at the rate of twelve or so to the acre in one of the fast-growing outer suburbs like Brentford or Greenford. If he was not fortunate enough to possess the modest means that this required, he might live in one of the new flats being put up by the London County Council to replace some of the worst slums, or on one of the council housing estates in the suburbs that were just beginning to show some consciousness of landscaping. If, as was likely, he did not embark on a large family, he would be able to afford a three-piece suite of living-room furniture in one of the latest designs and almost certainly, as time went on, a wireless. One piece of furniture that conferred some status was a cocktail cabinet, designed for the new drinking habits that were imported from America in the twenties. All of these items were available on hire purchase, a system of selling that came to favour during the thirties.

Furniture making has always been a characteristic London trade, and during the thirties it was relatively unaffected by the economic doldrums. One policy of the modernist movement was to produce designs suitable for mass production and for use in many different types of houses. The modified influence of both art deco and modernism was visible in countless London homes,

from the sunray motifs on garden gates and the fronts of wireless sets to the stepped fireplaces in the Aztec temple style and the geometric shapes of armchairs and sofas. Popular furnishing fabrics included floral chintzes and cottons printed with motifs of clouds or running deer, themes that were repeated in countless ornamental figurines, along with nubile girls, their hair flowing in the wind.

6 *Electric washing machine, 1931*

7 *Kitchen display at the Royal Arsenal Cooperative Society exhibition, November 1937*

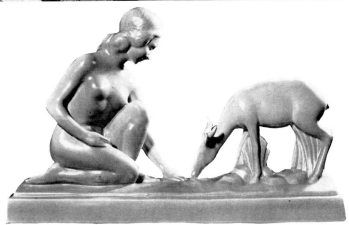

8 *Almond green china ornament*

9 Mantel-piece clock

10 Loudspeaker,
veneered in walnut

11 Electric fire,
green with silver
detail and a green
plastic handle

12 Cocktail cabinet, c 1937, veneered in bird's-eye maple

13 A typical pair of semi-detached suburban houses

14 Interior of the New Victoria cinema

15 A London street musician imitates Charlie Chaplin

HAPPY HIKING

3ᴰ

COMBINED
RAIL & WALKING
TOURS BY LMS

R&B

16 'Rambles round London', an LMS guide to Home Counties walks

Now that so many more people found a home of their own and the means to furnish it were within their reach, there were increasing attractions to a leisure spent at home. In 1939 nine out of every ten families in Britain owned a wireless set. Advertisers were quick to exploit the newer aspects of home life, and there was a steady growth of interest in parlour games, gardening and home decorating. The general interest in health and fitness boosted other cheap and wholesome pursuits like bicycling, swimming and hiking. One of the London County Council's proud boasts was of the number of new swimming baths and recreation grounds that it had provided; and this was the decade when the city's planners finally awoke to the need for a Green Belt. The pleasures of rural life ranked high amongst Londoners' enjoyments.

For the more urban minded, numerous choices presented themselves. The old music halls had declined by now into variety palaces. Their former audiences transferred their allegiance to the cinemas whose lavish décor often provided as much of an escape from reality as the films themselves. In 1930 the Talkies were in their infancy, from which they emerged to an adolescence of extravagance, exuberance and glamour. Despite financial difficulties and a general preference for Hollywood stars like Chaplin and Greta Garbo, a British film industry developed. Alexander Korda tried to meet the American challenge by out-doing Hollywood; his studios at Denham were lavishly equipped and his productions invariably overran their budgets. *The Private Life of Henry VIII* (1933) raised Charles Laughton to the popularity of a Hollywood idol and its financial success attracted large-scale investment in the film industry. In 1936 more than two hundred feature films were completed at London studios, but Henry VIII's successors fell short of expectations. There were other sides to the film industry, however. In 1935 *The Thirty Nine Steps* established Alfred Hitchcock's reputation, and *The Lady Vanishes*, made in Islington in 1937, was one of his most exciting films. Other attractions of the cinema included comedies starring Gracie Fields, George

13

Formby and Will Hay, and some less widely recognised but far-reaching developments in documentary film making under the inspiration and guidance of John Grierson and Sir Stephen Tallents.

Despite the fact that several London theatres including the Leicester Square trio of Daly's, the Empire and the Alhambra made way for cinemas, the decade was in many ways auspicious for West End theatre. Audiences revelled in the brittle sophistication of Noël Coward or of Rattigan's *French Without Tears* and in Housman's *Victoria Regina*, which appeared in coronation year. They flocked to the latest Cochran revue or Ivor Novello extravaganza at Drury Lane. The more serious theatre was still dominated by Bernard Shaw who, in his seventies, was as prolific and provocative as ever. And there were new dramatists: Emlyn Williams, whose psychological exploration of a murderer's reactions in *Night Must Fall* made the play a minor classic; and J. B. Priestley, preoccupied with theories of time in *Time and the Conways* and *I Have Been Here Before*. It was a good decade for the classics too: Peggy Ashcroft, John Gielgud and Lawrence Olivier were among the young actors making their names in Shakespearian revivals; and meanwhile the Old Vic under Lilian Baylis's management and Tyrone Guthrie's direction led the field in English classics and in more recent European masters like Ibsen and Chekhov. The one-time home of melodrama in Waterloo Road had progressed through the stages of music hall and temperance hall, and gained stature during the twenties and thirties as the home of serious drama. It was not without justice that, questioned in 1937 about proposals for a National Theatre, Lilian Baylis retorted that the Old Vic *was* the national theatre. This formidable woman, not content with her repertory of opera and plays in the Waterloo Road, also undertook the rebuilding of Sadler's Wells in Islington, and soon after the theatre was opened in 1931 added the presentation of ballet to her other responsibilities. Under the direction of Ninette de Valois the Vic-Wells ballet developed before the end of the decade into a fully-fledged company with an international reputation, and broke into a field hitherto dominated by the Russians.

In the world of classical music Sir Henry Wood was still master of the Proms, and from 1927 onwards the BBC sponsored his annual seasons at the Queen's Hall (which was demolished by bombing in May 1941). London frequently welcomed foreign musicians: Furtwängler, Rachmaninoff, Stravinsky and Toscanini, whose fearsome reputation struck terror in the hearts of the new BBC Symphony Orchestra when he first arrived to conduct them in a Brahms concerto. With the catalyst of broadcasting and the enthusiastic guidance of some great conductors, British music itself grew in confidence. The London Symphony Orchestra was reconstituted in 1929; in 1930 the BBC Symphony Orchestra gave their first performance under Adrian Boult and soon rose to international standing; and in 1932 the redoubtable Sir Thomas Beecham founded the London Philharmonic Orchestra. At Covent Garden, opera and ballet seasons alternated. The appearance of Colonel de Basil's Ballets Russes at the Alhambra in 1933 and afterwards at Covent Garden resurrected an enthusiasm for the Russian ballet that had seemed destroyed after the deaths of Diaghilev and Pavlova.

This was a great age for jazz, and indeed for almost any musical import from America. At fashionable clubs and parties American jazz groups were much in demand. Dance bands played the latest hits from Hollywood movies, songs made popular by Bing Crosby, Fred Astaire and a host of other names. Dancing was enormously popular, whether in Mecca dance halls or at fashionable private parties, and schools of dancing made their livings out of the quick-step, the fox-trot and the tango. It was rare for Londoners to find themselves dancing a new step of London origin, but in the winter of 1937-8 Lupino Lane's musical 'Me and My Girl' became a hit, and suddenly people were doing the Lambeth Walk, 'any where, any day' up to and after the outbreak of war. *Picture Post* published an article on the original Lambeth Walk, then a lively market street, and made much of the way the London character lent itself to such affectionate pastiche. The traditional Cockney way of life still flourished with undimmed vigour. In the East End and along the southern riverside in Bermondsey and Lambeth, people spoke with the distinctive accent and rhyming slang that amounted to a Cockney dialect. The colour and clamour of the street markets, the uproarious gaiety of evenings spent in pubs or dance-halls, somehow compensated for the dirt and poverty that were ingrained in the Cockney existence.

Apart from a mutual interest in dancing and some other recreations, London's high society existed in a world apart from

*17 In a 'poor man's shelter' in Wembley, posters advertise
greyhound and speedway racing*

the street markets and the dance halls. The 'season' continued fundamentally the same as it had been in the Edwardian era, with the obligatory round of balls, the presentations at court, the agonisings over invitation lists, the search for eligible young men, and above all the colossal expense. Evelyn Waugh calculated that it might cost a thousand pounds or more to launch a debutante; and that did not allow for the hire of a peeress to introduce her to all the right people. The great hostesses sparkled in their firmament, exciting the homage of their male guests and the envy of their women friends. They included the beautiful Lady Diana Cooper and the ageing Emerald Cunard. Lady Honor Channon was photographed for *Vogue* wearing an evening gown of classical simplicity and standing in the newly decorated blue rococo dining room of her Berkeley Square house. The accolade for such a hostess was to entertain the Prince of Wales (better still when he was King), to whom the young Duke and Duchess of Kent came a popular and glamorous second.

One of the obsessions of the decade was with speed, an interest that everyone could share, whether as spectator or participant. There was greyhound racing at Wembley, White City and Stamford Bridge, or motor-cycle racing at Crystal Palace; and Sir Malcolm Campbell's solo land speed records in 'Bluebird' excited great admiration. But the real headline stealer was aviation, as popular in the thirties as it had been in the twenties, or perhaps even more so. For two-and-sixpence apiece, Londoners could take flight from Northolt aerodrome for a trip over the city. There were flying clubs all over the country, and if any would-be aviator doubted whether his physical or financial capacities matched his ambition, there was the inspiring example of Amy Johnson, a secretary who joined the London Aeroplane Club at Stag Lane, Edgware in 1930 and flew solo from England to Australia in a Gipsy Moth. She went on to record many achievements that thrilled the British public and made her the heroine of the thirties. Other daring aviators included Amy's husband Jim Mollison, and Jean Batten, who flew to South Africa in record time in her tiny plane 'Jean'. That great eccentric the elderly Duchess of Bedford was reported missing over the south coast of England in 1936. And the Prince of Wales's interest set the seal of glamour on aviation. Air travel was a novelty experienced by very few, but there was something about the idea of aviation, a sense of escape, speed and adventure, that captured the imaginations of millions of land-bound people.

If your taste did not run to watching air displays or actually going up in a plane, you could get your thrills at a football match on a Saturday afternoon. The great London clubs of the thirties were Arsenal, Chelsea, Tottenham Hotspur and West Ham. Arsenal drew the largest crowds, and twice during the decade they rewarded their supporters by winning the FA cup at Wembley. The maximum wage for a footballer was fixed at eight pounds a week, and only a real star could expect to get that. Transfer fees were unknown, and the absence of floodlights meant that relatively few matches could be fitted into the season. Despite all that, a young player would count himself lucky in a time of very high unemployment to have a job that combined such challenge and excitement with what then seemed generous pay.

18 (above right) A London shop window advertises television in October 1936

19 (right) Girls in a milk bar, a new type of meeting-place in the thirties

20 (far right) Part of a queue that waited thirty-six hours for the opening of the 1930 opera season at Covent Garden

22 (above) A page from the winter sale catalogue of Barkers of High Street, Kensington, 1935

21 (left) Window shopping in Bond Street, 1937

23 (right) Street market in the Cut, Lambeth

25 (above) *Boys swimming in the Thames at Wapping*

24 (left) *Members of the Women's League of Health and Beauty at the Festival of Youth in Wembley Stadium, 5 July 1937*

The growing interest in sport owed something to a widespread concern for physical fitness in general. After the end of the First World War, the miserable health of most of the population received increasing attention. During the twenties, several acts were passed affecting public health, and people were urged to take a more positive attitude towards their own health. In 1929 Neville Chamberlain as Minister of Health steered an important Local Government Act through parliament whereby responsibility for hospitals and other medical institutions was transferred from the separate poor-law bodies that had formerly administered them to the local councils. Thus in London the LCC took charge of seventy-six hospitals and other institutions, with a total of forty-two thousand beds. The health of those who could not afford to pay medical bills was at last removed from its traditional association with indigence and charity to the sphere of normal local administration.

Health became something of a national fixation. Newspapers and magazines were cluttered with advertisements for pills and panaceas, for health-giving drinks, sunray lamps and keep-fit exercise machines. Every popular magazine had its regular feature on health. The Boy Scout movement had a world membership of three hundred and forty thousand in its jubilee year (1937); and the Women's League of Health and Beauty became popular and famous. With the number of sports clubs and recreation grounds in London increasing rapidly, provision for health and recreation became a leading issue in local and national elections.

In Parliament, the 'national health' was frequently the subject of discussion, above all when it related to housing and the problem of the slums. A Public Health Act in 1936, the Factories and Physical Training Acts of 1937 and Food and Drugs Act of 1938 all tackled aspects of the health problem, but too often shortage of money made serious difficulties all the more intractable. It was a time when abundant good intentions in the sphere of social reform often battled against overpowering economic and political necessities. There were, however, some advances in medical research and in the education of public opinion. Some progress was made in the battle against tuberculosis; and the First World War had helped to improve techniques of surgery. Between 1918 and 1939 there was a dramatic improvement in personal hygiene, very largely due to the fashions for skimpier clothes and a more active way of life. Fashion chased away the flea. Dietary habits also began to improve: scientists studied the nation's food consumption, and in 1933 the British Medical Association issued new standards for a minimum diet; the following year free school milk was introduced for the first time.

The Peckham Health Centre, opened in 1935, showed how a group of private individuals could put the latest ideas into practice, unhampered by any obligation to spread public money equally over all the areas of need. In their magnificent new building designed for two thousand families, the Peckham pioneers provided a pleasant club-like atmosphere and social facilities together with regular medical check-ups and provision for various forms of healthy exercise. Their scientific observation of the centre's members together with their belief in the overriding importance of the family unit, embodied two very noticeable trends of the thirties.

In Britain as a whole, the birth rate was declining seriously; it was estimated that by 1952 there would be more deaths than births each year. The population of greater London and the south-east was expanding, but the youth of the nation was at a premium wherever it might happen to live. In a decade when no youth culture existed such as we know today, and when fashions in clothes, entertainment and moral values all seemed to be set by an older generation, there was nonetheless a heavy emphasis on protecting and encouraging young people. A few months after the Olympic Games had been held in Berlin in 1936, a team of British observers went to Germany to investigate the merits and drawbacks of the 'Strength through Joy' campaign, the Nazi régime's massive organisation for training young Germans in physical fitness. The British team reported to Parliament with great enthusiasm, their only serious reservation being that the German system tended to encourage discipline at the expense of independent thought. Many of their recommendations were incorporated into a Physical Fitness Bill which was being debated in parliament in the same week when a Festival of Youth took place in Wembley Stadium in the presence of the King and Queen and the Princesses Elizabeth and Margaret Rose.

The Festival of Youth displayed a certain quality of optimism and innocence that belonged peculiarly to the thirties. A *Times* reporter rhapsodised on the theme: 'the young people were clad as for the day and, in their flimsy array, they marched forth to greet the sun and to gambol in its radiance.' As the representatives of some thirty national organisations for young people proudly marched, bicycled or cartwheeled past the royal dais, no hint of a troubled future nor echo of more sinister displays in Germany seemed to cloud the scene. In answer to the festival's critics, *The Times* referred to 'that disciplined vigour of the body which is the first security for the facing of moral and spiritual problems with the sane intelligence required of a free people.'

26 *Mother and children eat a snack beside the swimming pool at the Peckham Health Centre*

27 In the autumn of 1931 the new National Government pasted its own slogans over Conservative Party posters in preparation for the general election

The theme of youth and fitness played its part in politics as well as in the social life and recreations of the nation, and a strong vein of dissatisfaction with the older generation ran through political life. The men who ran the country were not (with few exceptions) of that age-group which had sacrificed so many men on the battlefields of Europe. Young politicians, bitterly aware that many of their most talented contemporaries had perished, felt that they belonged to a lost generation; such a holocaust must never be permitted to happen again.

For most electors and many politicians these memories engendered an obsession with peace and security. Determined that young people then growing up should never have to face the terror of war, the nation tried to ignore the threats that were mounting in continental Europe. Public opinion, often followed rather than led by the government, was desperate for peace. Both the National Government and its Labour and Liberal opponents showed a fondness for embellishing their election posters with pictures of small children: 'Their future is in your hands,' the electorate was reminded.

In fact, neither the National Government nor the depleted Labour and Liberal parties could offer a secure future for anyone. In 1929 Ramsay MacDonald formed his second Labour government in promising circumstances: unemployment, though it was still above the million mark, was lower than it had been for most of the twenties; the economy seemed relatively healthy; and a series of conferences and negotiations abroad offered hope for international disarmament and for the settlement of the Indian problem. But in October 1929 came the Wall Street crash. The disaster shook all of the world's leading economies. American loans for investment in industry ceased to flow, and the products of industry lost their outlet in American markets. The first wave of the Depression became a tide, as many millions of people were thrown out of work in Europe and America.

23

28 (above) The early days of the British Union of Fascists: eight hundred London fascists marched to Euston station on their way to hear Mosley speak in Manchester, October 1933

29 (left) In July 1933 thirty thousand Jews marched through London, starting at Stepney Green, to protest against the Nazi regime in Germany. These were some of the rabbis in the procession

30 (above right) Communists give the clenched fist salute from behind a barricade in Lambeth

Since the First World War, English bankers had been struggling to maintain the position of London as financial capital of the world; and to this end they lent large sums of money, mainly to German banks, at high rates of interest. When the famous Credit-Anstalt bank in Vienna found itself unable to meet its obligations, it set off a chain reaction in Germany, which rapidly had an effect in London. If the German banks repudiated their debts, then the British banks could not meet theirs. It was the sudden collapse of confidence in Britain's ability to pay her debts that forced the Labour government to consider a set of extremely harsh measures.

Lack of confidence was at the root of Britain's dilemma, and It was a lack of daring that made MacDonald choose the solution that he did. The terror of inflation hung over the government, even though prices were actually falling; and they were, moreover, under immense pressure to find a traditional solution.

MacDonald's position was further weakened by the general distrust of a Labour government, which was still a novelty readily suspected of financial incompetence. He and his Chancellor of the Exchequer, Philip Snowden, joined forces with Liberal and Conservative leaders to form a 'National Government' that could push stringent economies through parliament. Income tax was raised to five shillings in the pound, all salaries and wages paid by the state were cut by ten per cent, and unemployment pay, the greatest source of 'waste' according to Labour's critics, also fell by ten per cent. These remedies proving insufficient, the new government finally devalued the pound, the one measure that they had sworn to prevent.

In November 1931, having rescued the country from an emergency that very few people really understood, the newly formed National Government appealed to the electorate for a 'doctor's mandate'. They faced a general election without any

25

specific programme, but relied on their reputation as saviours of the country for the authority to go on saving it from the evils of the Depression. Some Labour MPs and some Liberals adhered to the coalition, but it was the Conservative Party that provided the bulk of its support. Ramsay MacDonald's broadcast to the electors that November sounded like a plea for understanding: 'It was a hard thing to do, but it had to be done.' The electors, it seemed, did understand; but the Labour Party neither understood nor forgave; MacDonald and his colleagues Snowden and J. H. Thomas were thrown out of the party.

If the times called for visionary leadership, there were those who thought they could provide it. Sir Oswald Mosley left the Labour Party in disgust when it rejected his expansionist proposals for the economy; and in 1931 he formed the New Party to promote an economic policy that in many ways resembled the New Deal later implemented in America by Roosevelt. The New Party rapidly disintegrated for lack of any unifying set of convictions, and in October 1932 Mosley founded the British Union of Fascists. Still quite a young man, his sense of disillusionment with older politicians, together with his own meteoric rise to success, made him feel not only that Britain was crying out for a dynamic new leader but that he himself was destined to be that leader. He became interested in Mussolini and the economic miracle that fascism seemed to be bringing about in Italy; and by the middle of 1932 the Italian dictator had converted the former great white hope of the British Labour Party to fascism.

The British Union of Fascists never won a seat in parliament, and its membership never spread beyond a tiny minority of the population; but it brought into national politics a new note of fervent patriotism or sinister nationalism, depending on how you looked at it. The militaristic and violent sides of the movement were those that developed most conspicuously. At mass meetings held in the Albert Hall and at Olympia and Earl's Court, dissenters were weeded out of the audience by violent officials. Roars of applause greeted the entry of the speakers, who were escorted to the platform by jack-booted members of the Division I Blackshirts; and Mosley, speaking last, conducted the meeting in a crescendo of enthusiasm. The movement found its greatest strength in the East End of London. It was there that it chose to concentrate its campaign in local government

elections and even managed, in 1937, to win more than nineteen per cent of the vote (but no seats). There too, it found the ideal victim of nationalist sentiment: the Jews.

East End Jews, living mainly in Whitechapel, were the target for much resentment. The great majority of Jewish families had fled from Russia during the pogroms at the end of the nineteenth century; and although the young adults of the thirties had been born and brought up as Londoners, their neighbours still regarded them as alien. Some of them lived in abject poverty, excluded by prejudice from the more secure jobs and suffering as much as any other group from the general scarcity of work. But many more fortunate Jews were shopkeepers or tailors, and their relative prosperity excited envy. The letters P. J. (Perish Judah) began to appear on synagogue walls, and Jewish tradesmen found themselves systematically harassed. On 5 October 1936 Mosley's forces clashed head-on with the combined opposition of Jews and communists. The 'battle of Cable Street' forced Mosley to disperse his parade of Blackshirts in their new uniforms, and a week later fascist supporters retaliated with the 'Mile End pogrom', smashing Jewish shop windows and assaulting Jews in the streets. It was one of the most violent weeks in London's history; and it marked the highest point in fascist strength.

As a result of these terrors an outraged Parliament hastened to pass the Public Order Act, which banned the wearing of political uniforms in public and gave the Commissioner of Police power to ban processions or marches that seemed likely to cause a breach of the peace. Although Mosley claimed that his audience of thirty-nine thousand at Earl's Court in July 1939 constituted the largest mass meeting in British history, membership of the British Union of Fascists and National Socialists (so named since 1936) declined as war approached. In May 1940, under Defence Regulation 18b, Sir Oswald Mosley was arrested and imprisoned, and his party was banned.

East London, giving strength to fascism, also became a natural home for communism. In few other parts of Great Britain did politics polarise so sharply. For many young Jews the Communist Party seemed to be their obvious defence; and there were plenty of other people sufficiently revolted by the outrages of the BUF to turn to its extreme opposite, or who felt that only the Communist Party offered a way out of the poverty and squalor of the slums. Outside the East End and the poorer parts of South London, the Communist Party commanded strong support from intellectuals. Its national membership climbed from under one-and-a-half thousand in 1930 to more than ten times that number in 1938, and reached a peak of over fifty-five thousand during the Second World War. Until the outbreak of war, communists were always outnumbered by fascists, but under the leadership of Harry Pollitt and R. Palme Dutt they developed a far-reaching propaganda system and won much sympathy from the left wing in general. With its influence in trade unions and amongst tenants' associations and other pressure groups, the Communist Party could claim to have affected British politics more deeply than the British Union of Fascists had done. And the election propaganda of both the Conservative and the Labour parties suggested that fear of communism was more potent than fear of the fascists.

London's politics differed from those of the rest of the country, not only in the support that the city gave to the extremes of left and right, but also in providing a stronghold for the Labour Party at a time when its position in the country was weak. Many London constituencies returned Labour MPs, several of whom were among the party leadership: George Lansbury, Clement Attlee and Herbert Morrison. And in 1934, Labour won control of the London County Council for the first time. They were not to lose it again until after the LCC became the Greater London Council in 1963. The LCC enjoyed its heyday during the thirties, and Morrison described the time that he spent as its leader as 'one of the happiest and most inspiring phases of [his] life.' During these years the LCC increased its programme of slum clearance and rehousing, and pioneered the Green Belt. It could also boast of smaller triumphs such as the replacement of the old Waterloo Bridge by a new and stronger one, a *cause célèbre* of London in the thirties. The Labour members of the LCC formed the most widely respected section of their party,

31 (above right) Hunger marchers from Norwich marching through Stratford, East London, in October 1932

32 (right) The flag of the British Battalion of volunteers on the republican side in the Spanish Civil War

perhaps because they were among the few who had a chance for positive action.

Lacking unity and credibility at home, the left in British politics received constant stimulus from events on the continent: from the menace of Nazi Germany and from the French and Spanish examples of a 'Popular Front' that united all parties of the left to fight against fascism. In the autumn of 1936, war broke out between the elected Popular Front government of Spain and the right-wing forces of the Falange. It soon became a crusade for people all over the world. Those who hit the headlines were the members of the International Brigade, men drawn from all walks of life who went to fight on the Republican side. Other supporters of the Republican cause sent lorry loads of supplies, or helped to raise funds at home. There were Englishmen fighting on both sides, and for many of them the war embodied a struggle against evil, whether communist or fascist, that they could not find at home. On the Republican side, the poetry of Auden, Spender and MacNiece and the journalism of Claud Cockburn and others brought home to British readers the intensity of feeling that the war aroused. The depleted International Brigade dispersed to its various countries of origin at the end of 1938, defeated and disillusioned. Many of its members and some of those who had gone more to observe than to fight found that their experiences in Spain had disenchanted them for ever with the notion of a just war. They could view with wearied detachment the far greater struggle that was looming near.

In Britain, the Popular Front existed not in a coalition of political parties but in the shape of the Left Book Club. Founded by the publisher Victor Gollancz in 1936, the club aimed to unite liberals, socialists and communists in the fight against fascism. Gollancz wanted to supply left-wing literature that everyone could afford; and for two-and-sixpence a month the club's members received the monthly selection, bound in limp orange covers. Within a year, almost forty-five thousand people had joined, and the Left Book Club established discussion groups, a left-wing theatre company and the influential monthly _Left News_. As a publishing venture, it was amazingly successful and much imitated; as a political experiment, it provided an invaluable forum for dissent and discussion. But the political conditions out of which it grew changed abruptly at the end of 1939. The pact between Nazi Germany and Soviet Russia at the beginning of the Second World War caused a split in the British left in general; and the idea of a popular front became obsolete.

Despite the success of the Left Book Club and the growing membership of the Communist Party, the great majority of the population remained moderate and conservative throughout the decade. In striking contrast to the unstable politics of France and Spain and the dictatorships of Germany and Italy, the British electorate returned a Conservative-dominated National Government by large majorities at both the general elections of the decade. In 1935 Stanley Baldwin succeeded Ramsay MacDonald, with his slogan 'Safety First.' This note of caution has been said to typify Britain in the thirties. But behind the seeming apathy there lay some profound uncertainties. Most people found their material circumstances improving gradually, but the spectre of unemployment and slump haunted the political scene. Hunger marchers from the 'distressed areas' brought grim reminders of their problems; and in the November rain of 1936 the Jarrow marchers, most famous of them all, trudged through London's streets led by their MP 'red' Ellen Wilkinson, after weeks spent on the road. The number of unemployed declined between 1934 and 1937, but it never fell below a million, and in 1937 it began to rise again. About a third of working-class families were still living below the bread line at the end of the decade, and nothing that the government did seemed to help. Other fears pressed in from abroad. Peace was the slogan of all the political parties, but its maintenance became more and more precarious. With each advance made by Hitler or Mussolini: into the Rhineland, into Abyssinia and eventually into Czechoslovakia, the British government appeared more ineffectual and less honourable. Public opinion only compounded their difficulties. The Labour Party, led by George Lansbury and then by Clement Attlee, campaigned for peace at almost any price. And in 1935 the Reverend Dick Sheppard, canon of St. Martin-in-the-Fields, founded the Peace Pledge Union, attracting a membership of one hundred and thirty thousand by 1937. Such a number dwarfed the membership of any other movement. The newspaper press added its voice almost unanimously to the call for peace, failing to understand, as did almost everyone else, that peace was not a Nazi objective and that both appeasement and isolation were therefore doomed to fail.

33 At the end of September 1938 the country trembled on the brink
of war. The Prime Minister is seen here about to leave for a second
conference with Hitler, in Munich. It was from this journey that he
returned with 'peace with honour'

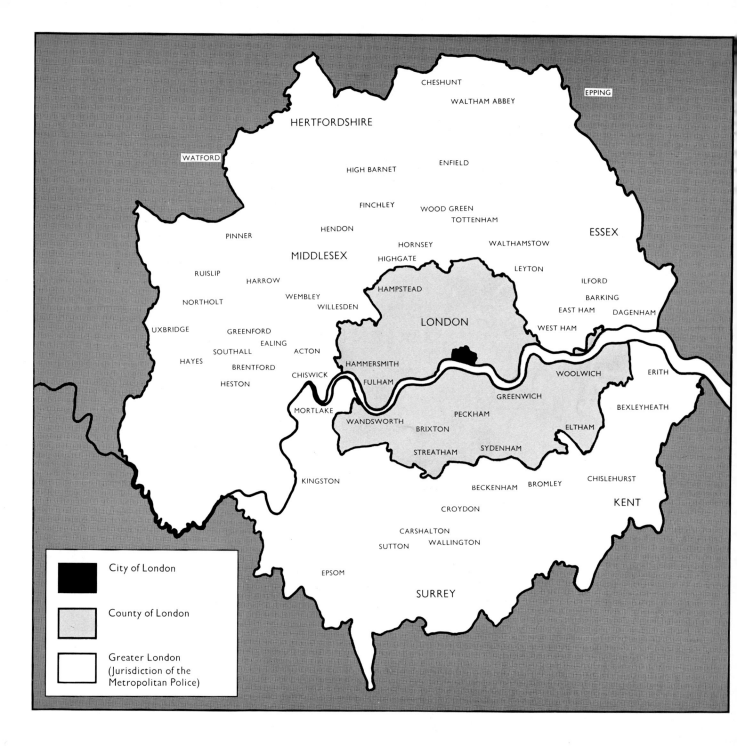

CHESHUNT

EPPING

WALTHAM ABBEY

HERTFORDSHIRE

WATFORD

HIGH BARNET

ENFIELD

FINCHLEY

WOOD GREEN

TOTTENHAM

HENDON

PINNER

ESSEX

MIDDLESEX

HORNSEY

WALTHAMSTOW

HIGHGATE

LEYTON

RUISLIP

HARROW

HAMPSTEAD

ILFORD

NORTHOLT

WEMBLEY

BARKING

WILLESDEN

LONDON

EAST HAM

DAGENHAM

UXBRIDGE

GREENFORD

WEST HAM

EALING

ACTON

WOOLWICH

ERITH

SOUTHALL

HAMMERSMITH

HAYES

BRENTFORD

CHISWICK

FULHAM

GREENWICH

BEXLEYHEATH

HESTON

MORTLAKE

WANDSWORTH

PECKHAM

ELTHAM

BRIXTON

STREATHAM

SYDENHAM

KINGSTON

CHISLEHURST

BECKENHAM

BROMLEY

KENT

CROYDON

CARSHALTON

EPSOM

SUTTON

WALLINGTON

SURREY

City of London

County of London

Greater London
(Jurisdiction of the
Metropolitan Police)

LONDON GROWS

35 (above) *A London United trolley-bus*

34 (left) *Suburbs and administrative boundaries of London during the thirties. The Metropolitan Police district was used to define Greater London and extended over an area of approximately fifteen miles' radius from Charing Cross. The Greater London of the seventies covers a slightly smaller area and is defined by the jurisdiction of the Greater London Council*

Throughout this troubled decade London was growing and changing rapidly. The area covered by the County of London itself was largely built-up by 1914; and after the First World War people began to move outside it, into new suburbs in Essex, Kent, Middlesex and Surrey. In 1939 the population of this new 'Greater London' was close to nine million, a peak from which it has been declining since the early fifties. About one fifth of all the people in Great Britain lived within a radius of fifteen miles from Charing Cross.

There was a building boom in most parts of the country, but nowhere was it so marked as in London's suburbs. A considerable amount of new building went on in established areas like Acton and Willesden, Wimbledon and the working-class districts of Enfield and Tottenham; and newer suburbs grew fast in north and west Middlesex and in parts of Surrey and Essex. At a time of economic uncertainty, land and houses were a popular investment. Building societies dropped the rates of interest that they charged on mortgages to around five per cent, and frequently entered into arrangements whereby they helped to finance the development of housing estates. One large London company offered houses for eight hundred pounds on payment of a twenty-five pound deposit, with all the legal expenses paid by the builder. The typical suburban house of the thirties was smaller and more streamlined than its precursors, catering for the smaller families and lower incomes of a new class of house buyers. Greater uniformity of building materials helped firms to build more quickly; and in its peak years one firm frequently completed as many as twelve houses per week on one estate.

This rapid growth did not always lead to the happiest results. 'Ribbon development' alongside new arterial roads like the North Circular and Western Avenue created rows of houses that stared out at each other across a sea of traffic. It was the accepted wisdom that people were better off in separate or at least semi-detached houses each with its own little garden. But the need for shops and services at a convenient distance was sometimes forgotten; and notions of planning to create some sense of community gave way, if they were considered at all, to the urgency of the builders' and buyers' need for land.

Despite a general growth of interest in town planning that dated back to the beginning of the century, there was little progress in planning for London. The Greater London Regional Planning Committee, founded in 1927, had no power to control the whims of builders and property developers. Their one great success was to persuade the LCC to launch a Green Belt scheme in 1935. The council proposed to make grants to neighbouring county councils to preserve land for recreation, and were prepared to spend as much as two million pounds over three years. In just over a year they were promised more than twenty-eight square miles mostly in Buckinghamshire, Essex and Middlesex, and had procured legislation to safeguard them against harmful development. It was the beginning of a policy that would eventually create a girdle of parkland around London and protect more than fifty-six square miles against new building.

Meanwhile, the poorest Londoners stayed behind in the slums close to the centre. The general movement out to the suburbs in no way helped them; and it was they who were affected by the acute shortage of housing that the city faced throughout the decade. Judged by the rather crude standard of 'overcrowding' defined in the Housing Act of 1935, the worst areas were in Shoreditch, Bethnal Green, Finsbury, Stepney, Bermondsey, Poplar, Southwark, St. Pancras and Islington. But every London borough had its corners of poverty. Between 1930 and 1939 the LCC declared well over three hundred acres of slums to be clearance areas, involving the homes of some seventy thousand people.

Both the LCC and the borough councils rehoused tens of thousands of people during the decade in new blocks of flats or on cottage estates. But many slum dwellers dreaded the visits of the overcrowding inspectors, who might force them to move to council flats that were more expensive than their original homes, and where they would not be allowed to carry on business on the premises. No tailor or cabinet-maker earning a precarious living in his own home, or casual worker whose wife

eked out his wages by taking in washing or sewing, could contemplate such a move. The job that the councils faced was formidable; and it was not even half done when war broke out and the destruction of the slums was left to the haphazard cruelties of the blitz.

Away from both slums and suburbs, the centre of London was not enjoying a very felicitous period in its architectural history. The majority of English architects conceded little to the latest developments on the continent, but failed to develop an effective style of their own. When Walter Gropius, founder of the Bauhaus, spent the first four years of his exile in England he received very few commissions. In London the only examples of his work are a house in Church Street, Chelsea and a film laboratory at Denham, in both of which he cooperated with the English architect and designer Maxwell Fry. Two well-known public buildings of the thirties, Broadcasting House in Portland Place and the Senate House behind the British Museum,

36 Advertisement for suburban houses in the early thirties

37 (right) An aerial view of the Crystal Palace in its south London home, where it had been transferred from Hyde Park in the 1850's. In November 1936 it burned down; the flames could be seen from as far afield as Highgate, and thousands of people drove to Sydenham to watch the destruction of a historic landmark

illustrate the decade's more usual style. Pale and monolithic, both show signs of classical influence in keeping with the areas into which they intruded, but it is an influence struggling with only partial success to come to terms with the demands of new materials, new institutions and a new scale.

Some of the most successful new buildings in London were built for commercial and industrial purposes: cinemas, for example, whose art deco interiors are now again arousing keen interest; or less spectacularly, some new department stores in Oxford Street and Kensington, and in particular the Peter Jones building in Sloane Square designed by William Crabtree. Giles Gilbert Scott's design for Battersea Power Station, now a familiar landmark, aroused strong feelings when it first appeared, but successfully set the standard for later power stations. And amongst the new factories springing up in Middlesex were some superbly imaginative examples of industrial self-confidence. Never before has a style stamped itself so daringly on industrial building as did art deco on, for example, the Hoover factory in Perivale (opened in 1933) or the Firestone plant beside the Great West Road (1928).

Partly because of its large labour supply, London had always been, and it remained, the chief manufacturing centre of the country. Between the wars, new industries grew up in new parts of the London area, which helped to change the pattern of the city's life. By 1932 the Ford Motor Company was employing seven thousand people at its new factory in Dagenham; and in west Middlesex thousands found work in factories that made either vehicles or vehicle parts or tyres. Another expanding industry was electrical engineering, concentrated especially in Woolwich to the east and in Acton, Hayes, Harlington and Wembley to the west. In Woolwich they specialised in making heavy cables; elsewhere it was everything from vacuum cleaners to wireless sets, ignition machinery and electrical accumulators. Various other engineering works flourished in the Lea valley to the north of Dagenham, along the banks of the river, in Croydon and in west Middlesex. Some of the longer established industries were also changing their habits and moving to the outer fringes of London. Furniture makers, for instance, were to be found in Tottenham, Edmonton and Walthamstow. A few printing works moved away from the inner area, although the newspaper press and the book trade

kept most of them close to the centre. And some new clothing factories were set up outside central London, in particular those that specialised in making underwear and stockings.

The new factories encouraged changes that were already taking place in London's public transport, and which in their turn influenced the industrialists' choice of sites. Under the aegis of the London Passenger Transport Board, London Transport's predecessor, the Bakerloo underground line was extended to Stanmore and the Piccadilly line to Cockfosters. Motor bus services linked stations with their surroundings, and steadily superseded the trams. In South London, the newly electrified lines of the Southern Railway discouraged the development of tube lines (except for the Northern Line's extension to Morden and promoted an increase in long-distance commuting from the towns of Kent, Surrey, Sussex and the South Coast.

39 (above) An aerial view of the Firestone
Factory on the Great West Road, before suburban
housing and other factories covered the fields
around it

38 (left) University of London: the Senate House
seen from Russell Square

40 (right) The Peter Jones building in
Sloane Square

PEOPLE AT WORK

43 *Travelling to work on the Underground*

41 (above left) The building of the blast furnace at the Ford factory in Dagenham, 1930

42 (left) A view of the Guinness brewery under construction in Park Royal, Middlesex, 1935

Apart from the changes in where people worked and lived and how they travelled between the two places, habits and conditions of work were beginning to change too. For one thing, the number of women at work was steadily increasing. The slaughters of the first world war had left a large proportion of women without husbands and in need of jobs. Before 1914 it had been unusual for women to work in offices even as clerks or typists; but by 1939 typing and secretarial work were regarded as their particular preserves. There was as yet, however, no conception of equal pay. In the civil service, generally regarded as a progressive employer, it was only at the end of the decade that women were granted eighty per cent of the salary of men doing identical jobs; and they were still compelled to leave work when they married.

The greatest improvement in working conditions was the spread of holidays with pay. In 1930 paid holidays were a rare privilege, but by 1938 some five million people were entitled to an annual holiday (usually a fortnight) with full pay. The credit for this triumph lay partly with the unions and partly with the employers' new understanding that leisure and recreation were essential to the health of their work force. Another major improvement came with the Factory Act of 1937, which laid down new safety standards and shortened the maximum working hours for women and young people. Despite this progress, employers were still not legally obliged to give compensation for injuries suffered at work, most industrial workers had to work on Saturdays, and the national average income remained below two hundred pounds a year. In London there were greater opportunities for employment than could be found elsewhere; but a large and increasing proportion of Londoners worked in the service industries, which were traditionally badly paid. Concentrated at the centre of the city, close to the hotels, cinemas and office blocks that gave them work, they were especially vulnerable to the high costs and poor housing of central London. Their poverty was shared by some workers in long-standing industries like the clothing trade, which could not compete with the wages offered by new and expanding businesses in the suburbs.

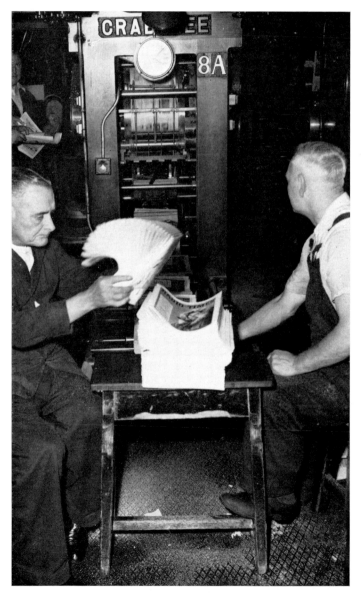

46 (above) Men and women making inner tubes for tyres at the Firestone factory

45 (above top) A Bayswater milkman

44 (left) Work on the Radio Times at the Waterlows factory in Park Royal, which opened in 1936

47 *East London girls working in the Royal Arsenal Cooperative
Society's preservatory during the strawberry season*

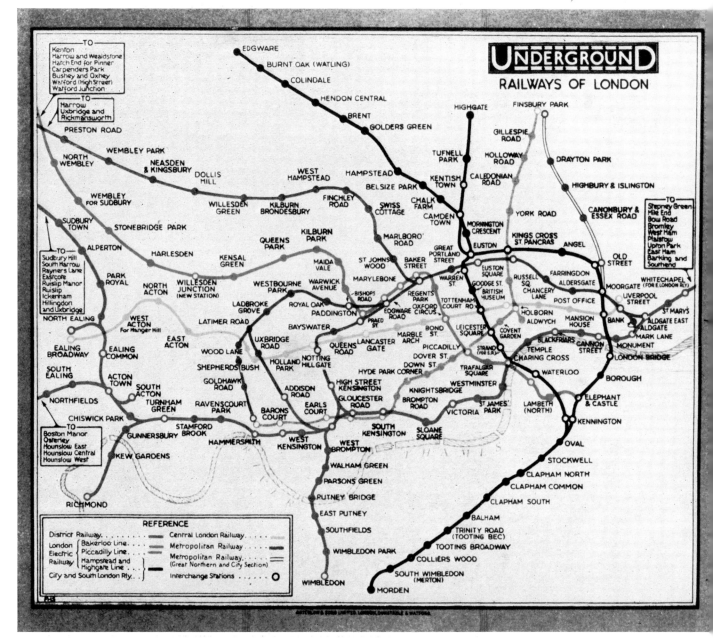

48 Map of London Underground Railways, c 1933

49 *Souvenir handkerchief for the silver jubilee of George V's reign*

Perhaps it is in the nature of modern capital cities that the extremes of wealth and poverty should be found together at the centre, encircled by a buffer state of suburbia. Whether or not it owed its problems as well as its advantages to the fact, London in the thirties was a capital city in the fullest sense.

It witnessed most of the decade's great events at close quarters. From the termini of the different railway companies people poured into London, abandoning their wirelesses to see for themselves the splendours of royal ceremony: the marriage of Princess Marina of Greece to the Duke of Kent; the silver jubilee of George V and Queen Mary; the coronation of George VI and Queen Elizabeth. And in the winter of 1936 many Londoners heard the news of Edward VIII's abdication with a sense of personal loss.

The great talking points of the time – unemployment, the safeguarding of empire, the Abyssinian question, fascism, Czechoslovakia; all these were aired many times in meeting places all over London, and most spectacularly at Earl's Court, the Albert Hall and Olympia, and in Hyde Park and Trafalgar Square. Through the decade Londoners became used, almost inured, to the sight of hunger marchers making their way to Hyde Park. And in October 1938 they themselves flocked to Heston airport on the city's western edge, or to Downing Street, to greet the Prime Minister on his return from Munich. From time to time the arrival of foreign dignitaries reminded them of London's importance in the world at large. Like an omen of changing times, Mahatma Gandhi visited the capital of the Empire for the Round Table Conference in 1931, when he stayed in the East End, attracting much attention in the press. In May 1937 heads of state from all over the world came to take part in the coronation festivities; and Neville Chamberlain, who had just become Prime Minister, presided over an Imperial Conference.

There were more solid reminders of the outside world. In South Kensington, a late Victorian pile housed the Imperial

50 (above) Crowds surround Amy Johnson at Croydon airport after her return from breaking the record speed for a flight to the Cape and back, 15 June 1936

51 (left) A bizarre reminder that London was still centre of a commercial as well as a political Empire. These elephants were paraded through part of the City one day in 1939 to celebrate the centenary of London's tea trade

52 (above right) Air mail, one of the new links between London and the rest of the world, was despatched from Croydon airport

53 (right) The new, streamlined Coronation Scot steams through Berkhampsted on its way to London, 1937

54 Londoners get the news of Edward VIII's abdication

55 One of the many souvenirs produced for Edward VIII's coronation, which was planned for 12 May 1937. In fact his brother George VI was crowned on that day

institute, where scientists carried out important research on methods of helping colonial economies. The wealthier dominions made their presence felt in imposing buildings like South Africa House in Trafalgar Square; and now they were also linked with London by air mail. The embassies dotted around the West End included the German one in Carlton House Terrace, where for two years Joachim von Ribbentrop was ambassador before returning to Germany to become Hitler's foreign minister. It was he who, at a party in 1937, greeted the King with the Nazi salute. Other and more tragic witnesses to Nazi policy came in the shape of Jewish refugees, sponsored by private individuals or by the Central British Fund and other relief organisations. From 1933 they came to London in a steady flow that in 1938-9 became a flood. Thousands went on to other parts of the world, but by the outbreak of war there were an estimated eighty thousand refugees in Great Britain, many of them living in North London.

They found refuge in what was for them almost the safest part of Europe. But as the decade drew to its close London shared the fears that were growing all over the world. Having dismembered Czechoslovakia, Hitler turned his attention to Poland: there was no longer any question of appeasement. The prospect of war became a certainty, and London and the other big cities of Britain made their preparations. Air Raid Precautions were speeded up; factories making all kinds of peaceful commodities were warned that they would have to turn to the manufacture of munitions; people brought out the gas masks that they had put away with a sigh of relief after Munich. And on 1st September 1939, as Nazi troops were marching into Poland, London's schoolchildren stood in bewilderment on the platforms of the city's railway stations, waiting for trains to take them to safety in the country. Two days later the British government declared war on Germany. The air-raid sirens sounded, and Londoners trooped into their shelters; but it turned out to have been a false alarm. They were to wait uneasily for months, wondering whether perhaps the worst might never happen, before finally the bombs fell and the assault on their city began.

56 (above right) King George VI acknowledges the cheers of the crowd with his mother Queen Mary and his daughter Princess Margaret Rose

57 (right) A souvenir of the coronation that actually took place

58 (right) A woman takes on work hitherto done by men, as part of the war effort

60 (far right) Boadicea in the black-out: the declaration of war enabled Londoners for the first time to see the streets and monuments of the capital by natural moonlight

59 (below) The evacuation of school children from Paddington station

FURTHER READING

Many good books have been written about the 1930s, and those that have helped in this brief study are too numerous to be listed here. But among them are some that the general reader may find particularly interesting. They include:

Ronald Blythe, *The Age of Illusion. England in the Twenties and Thirties* (Hamish Hamilton, 1963)

Noreen Branson and Margot Heinemann, *Britain in the Nineteen Thirties* (Weidenfeld and Nicholson, 1971)

G. D. H. and Margaret Cole, *The Condition of Britain* (Gollancz, 1937)

Robert Graves and Alan Hodge, *The Long Weekend. A Social History of Great Britain, 1918-1939* (Faber and Faber, 1940)

C. L. Mowat, *Britain Between the Wars. 1918-1940* (Methuen, 1955)

Julian Symons, *The Thirties: a dream revolved* (Cresset Press, 1960)

A. J. P. Taylor, *English History 1914-1945* (Oxford University Press, 1965)

ACKNOWLEDGEMENTS

We are grateful to the following for permission to reproduce photographs. Copyright rests with the owners listed below or with the London Museum.

The *Architectural Review*, 14, 40 and cover

B. T. Batsford Ltd., 3, 17, 20, 23, 37

British Leyland Motor Corporation Ltd., 1, 35

British Railways, 53, 59

The Communist Party of Great Britain, 30, 32 and cover

Conway Picture Library, 25, 60

The *Daily Mirror*, 56

Firestone Ltd., 39, 46, 58

Ford Motor Company Ltd., 41

Arthur Guinness and Company Ltd., 42

Mrs C. Levy, 4

Post Office, 52

Mrs E. MacMurray, 24

Mansell Collection, 15, 19, 21, 38, 43, 45 and cover

Radio Times Hulton Picture Library, 27, 28, 29, 31, 33, 50, 54 and cover

Royal Arsenal Cooperative Society, 7, 18, 47

Waterlows Ltd., Park Royal, 44

Wates Ltd., 13, 36

Printed in England for Her Majesty's Stationery Office by Ben Johnson & Co. Ltd., York   Dd 503897 K96   Designed by HMSO Graphic Desig